110 -2013

Fever in the Oceans

written and illustrated by Stephen Aitken

magic wagon

visit us at www.abdopublishing.com

Published by Magic Wagon, a division of the ABDO Group, 8000 West 78th Street, Edina, Minnesota 55439. Copyright © 2012 by Abdo Consulting Group, Inc. International copyrights reserved in all countries. All rights reserved. No part of this book may be reproduced in any form without written permission from the publisher.

Looking Glass Library™ is a trademark and logo of Magic Wagon.

Printed in the United States of America, North Mankato, Minnesota.
052011
092011
♻ This book contains at least 10% recycled materials.

Written and Illustrated by Stephen Aitken
Edited by Stephanie Hedlund and Rochelle Baltzer
Cover and interior layout and design by Abbey Fitzgerald

Library of Congress Cataloging-in-Publication Data

Aitken, Stephen, 1953-
  Fever in the oceans / written and illustrated by Stephen Aitken.
    p. cm. -- (Climate change)
  Includes index.
  ISBN 978-1-61641-672-0
  1. Ocean temperature--Juvenile literature. 2. Ocean-atmosphere interaction--Juvenile literature. 3. Climatic changes--Juvenile literature. I. Title.
  GC161.2.A38 2012
  551.69162--dc22
                              2011001874

Contents

Climate and the Ocean

The ocean affects Earth's climate in many ways. It takes in heat in summer and lets it out in winter. Half of the oxygen on Earth comes from the ocean.

HOT FACT: Oceans cover more than 70 percent of Earth's surface.

Water vapor rises from the ocean and forms clouds. Winds blow the clouds to the land. Water falls from clouds as rain and snow. This is called the water cycle.

COOL IDEA: The amount of water on Earth stays the same. Almost all is stored in the ocean.

Climate change is heating up the oceans. Weather around the world is becoming more extreme. Hurricanes and tornadoes strike more often.

HOT FACT: Extreme weather can cause flooding on islands and in low-lying areas.

In Hot Water

Phytoplankton are tiny ocean plants. They form the first link in the marine food chain. But warm ocean water is reducing their numbers. Whales and other animals may not have enough food if waters keep warming.

HOT FACT: The whale shark is the world's largest fish. It is over 50 feet (15 m) long! It feeds almost entirely on plankton.

Many types of coral die if ocean water gets too warm. Coral reefs are homes to many colorful fish and plants. Where will the fish and plants go if the reefs disappear?

COOL IDEA: Scientists are growing corals in nurseries so they can move them to restore damaged reefs.

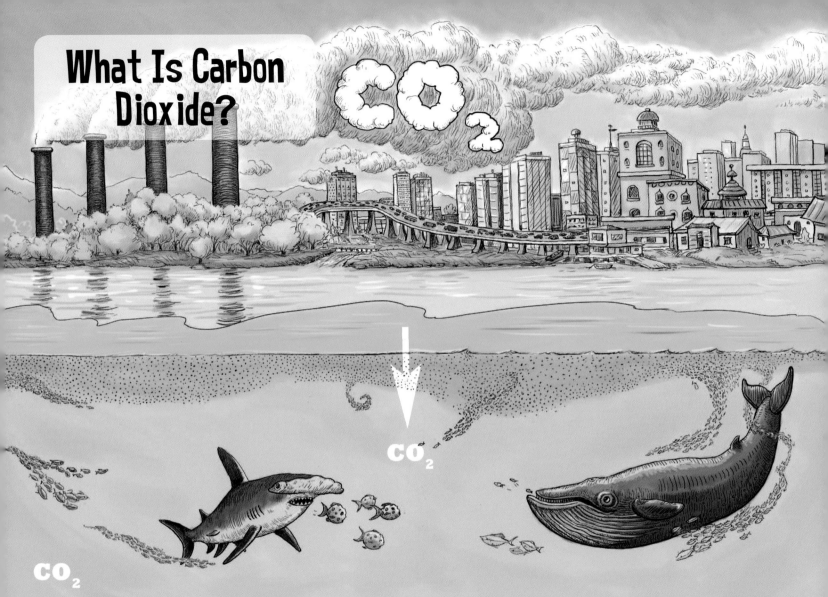

What Is Carbon Dioxide?

Carbon dioxide (CO_2) is a greenhouse gas. When it gets trapped in the atmosphere, it creates warmer temperatures.

14

Phytoplankton takes CO_2 from the air. It enters the food chain. Fewer phytoplankton means more CO_2 remains in the air.

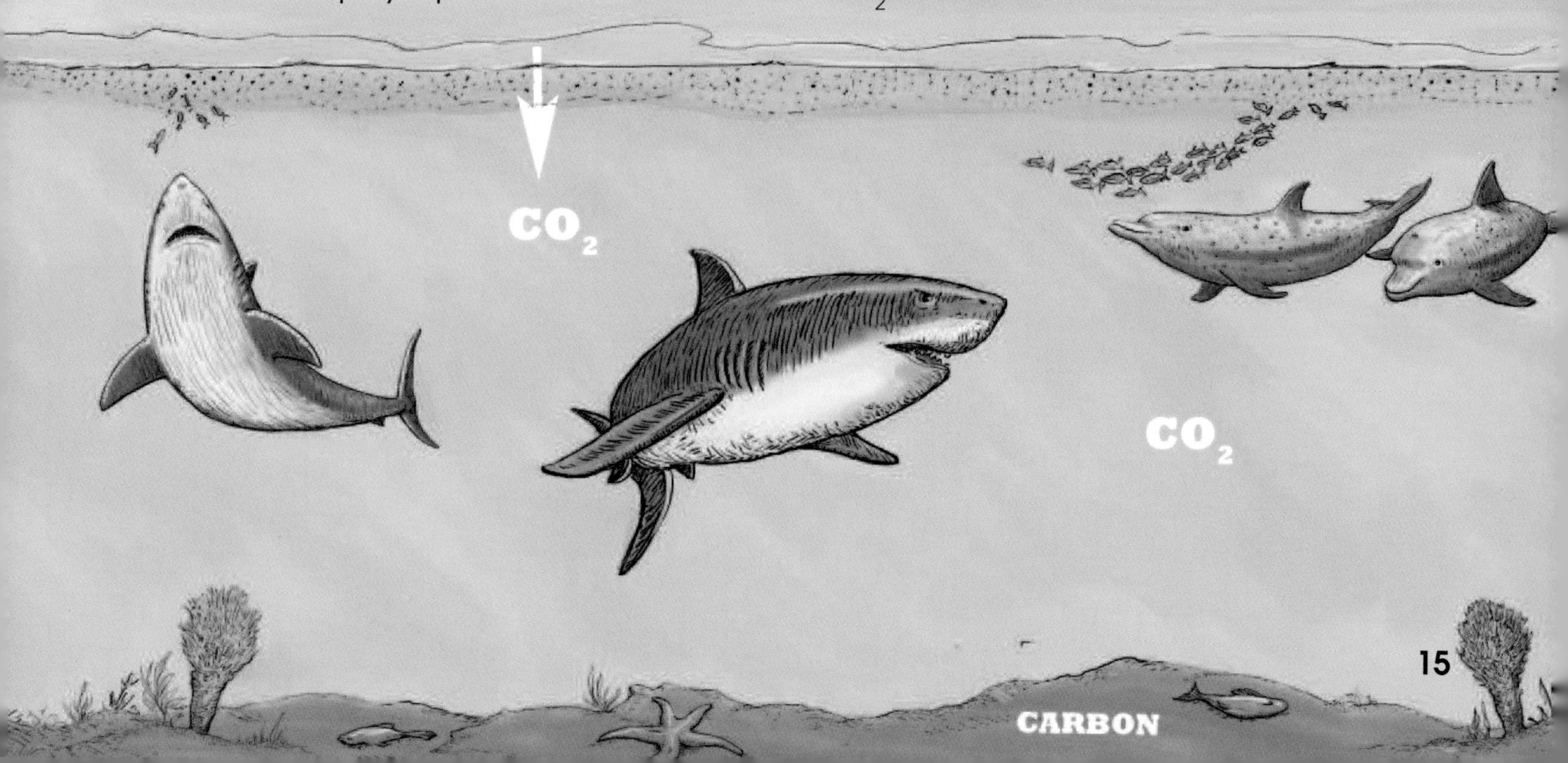

Over the past 200 years, the ocean has taken in a lot of CO_2. This is starting to change the water and hurt marine life. Studies show that plankton, corals, and shellfish now have thinner shells and skeletons.

CO₂

HOT FACT: Ocean water has changed more in the last 200 years than in the past 20 million years.

Melting Ice at the Poles

The oceans at the poles act like a refrigerator, cooling Earth. Temperatures at the poles are rising much faster than in the rest of the world. In 20 years, the Arctic Ocean may no longer have ice in the summer.

COOL IDEA: The health of ocean areas can be tracked by satellite through changes in color.

Because water is darker than ice, it absorbs more sunlight. As ice in the Arctic Ocean melts, the ocean heats up more quickly. Temperatures rise and the ground thaws. Buildings and houses on the frozen ground start to fall over.

COOL IDEA: Scientists drill long tubes of ice, called ice cores, from glaciers. They use the ice cores to study climate history.

Rising Sea Levels

When water is heated, it expands. This is the main reason sea levels rise.

Melting glaciers and ice sheets on land also add water to the ocean. Soon, many islands and coasts may be covered with water. People and wildlife could lose their homes.

HOT FACT: For every half inch (1 cm) the ocean rises, close to three feet (1 m) of coast is lost to the sea.

Protecting Oceans

Much of the land is protected by national parks and conservation areas. But, rising sea levels and extreme weather are causing erosion in coastal areas.

NATIONAL PARK

National Parks Service

NO HUNTING

HOT FACT: Less than five percent of the underwater world has been explored. Less than one percent is protected.

MARINE
Protected Area

COOL IDEA: The world's largest solar boat was built in 2008. It is powered entirely by the sun!

Rising water temperature is the biggest danger to ocean health. The best solution is to reduce the use of fossil fuels such as petroleum, natural gas, and coal. Renewable energy can help keep Earth *and* the oceans healthy!

Did You Know?

Wave power is a source of renewable energy. Scientists are now using waves to make electricity.

The level of carbon dioxide (CO_2) in the atmosphere is higher than it has been for at least 650,000 years.

An Austrian engineer has found a way to get power from whirlpools. This method might help avoid the need to build big dams on rivers.

The ocean takes in over 30 percent of the CO_2 created by human beings.

The Arctic tundra gives off methane gas when it melts. Methane is a greenhouse gas that is even more harmful than CO_2.

Scientists are making a fuel from pond scum. This fuel would not give off any additional CO_2 into the atmosphere.

Dr. Know, What Is Albedo?

Albedo is a measure of how much light an object reflects. A higher albedo means that more light is reflected and the object stays cooler, like ice and snow. Do you want to try an albedo experiment?

What you need:
- A black felt cloth
- A white felt cloth
- Aluminum foil
- A thermometer
- A heat lamp
- A notebook
- A pen
- A table

What to do:
1. Turn on the heat lamp and keep it 12 inches from the table.
2. Lay the thermometer on the table under the light and cover it with the black cloth. Allow it to heat for five minutes.
3. Write down the temperature of the thermometer and the type of cover.
4. Remove the thermometer and let it return to room temperature.
5. Repeat steps 2 to 4 with the white cloth.
6. Repeat steps 2 to 4 with the aluminum foil.

Which material reflected the most heat? Which material has the highest albedo? Which has the lowest albedo?

What Can You Do for the Ocean?

The change in Earth's temperature is almost totally due to human activities. People burning oil and gas for cars, trucks, and buses releases gases that trap heat on Earth. The power used to create electricity and other forms of energy adds to the problem. Here are a few things you can do to help keep the temperature from rising more!

Get active by talking about what you have learned in this book.

Many things you use can be used again. This is called recycling. You can recycle types of paper, plastic, and metals.

Find other people who want to help the ocean.

Make a list of things you use that cannot be recycled. Now see if you can replace these with things that can be recycled!

For one day try to recycle all of the things that you would normally throw out. Some of that waste could have ended up in the ocean.

Glossary

atmosphere - the layer of gas surrounding Earth.

carbon dioxide (CO_2) - a heavy, colorless gas that is formed when fuel that has the element carbon is burned.

conservation - the planned management of natural resources to protect them from damage or destruction. Conservation can also protect man-made resources, such as historic or cultural structures.

erosion - the wearing away of land, especially by wind or water.

food chain - the flow of energy from one living thing to the next.

greenhouse gas - a gas, such as carbon dioxide, that traps heat in Earth's atmosphere.

marine - related to the sea or ocean, including animals and plants.

plankton - small animals and plants that float in a body of water.

renewable energy - energy that can be replaced naturally. Renewable energy resources include wind energy and solar energy.

tundra - a vast, treeless plain in the Arctic. The ground beneath its surface is frozen all year long.

water vapor - tiny drops of water floating in the air.

Web Sites

To learn more about climate change, visit ABDO Group online at **www.abdopublishing.com**. Web sites about climate change are featured on our Book Links page. These links are routinely monitored and updated to provide the most current information available.

Index